LOVE
POEMS

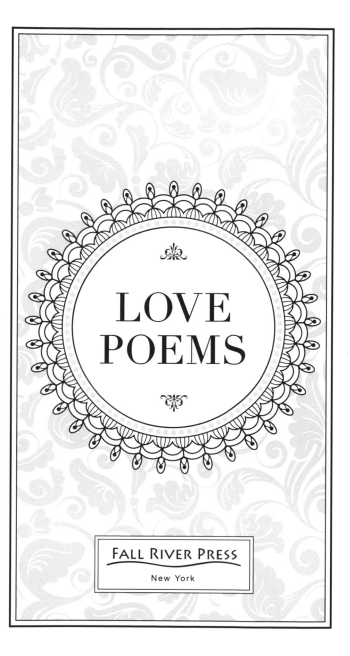

LOVE POEMS

FALL RIVER PRESS

New York

FALL RIVER PRESS

New York

An Imprint of Sterling Publishing
1166 Avenue of the Americas
New York, NY 10036

This compilation and its Introduction copyright © 2016
by Fall River Press.

Cover design by David Ter-Avanesyan

ISBN: 978-1-4351-6233-4

Manufactured in China

7 9 10 8 6

www.sterlingpublishing.com

CONTENTS

CONTENTS

CONTENTS

INTRODUCTION

THE LOVE POEM IS AS OLD AS THE POETIC tradition itself, and more poems have been written about love than on any other theme. This will come as no surprise to anyone who reads poetry— but neither should it surprise anyone who is *not* already familiar with the poems collected in this volume. For centuries, poetry was—many would say it still *is*—considered the noblest of literary forms, and romantic love the grandest of all poetic themes. The greatest poets rose to the challenge to put into words an emotion that all but defied expression— what Dante, in the poem translated here as "My lady carries love within her eyes," refers to as that which "cannot be said, nor holden in the thought." This anthology shows how some of the greatest poets of the last eight centuries succeeded in giving love a rich literary legacy.

The love lyrics collected here capture the many moods and temperaments of romantic love. Some express the ecstasy of being in love while others are more quiet and meditative. Some explore the general concept of romantic love while others are written in direct address to the poet's lover—indeed, several of these poems were their era's equivalent of love letters.

These poems also show the range of feelings that love provokes—not just passion and happiness, but also melancholy and frustration. Several poets regard romantic love as the apogee of human experience; others liken its intensity to that of religious devotion.

Virtually every poet who has put pen to paper has written a love poem, but some contributors to this volume are more surprising than others. Who would have thought that Matthew Gregory Lewis, author of the shocking gothic novel *The Monk,* could write a poem as tender as "I Never Could Love Till Now," or that the notoriously reclusive and reserved Emily Dickinson could write a stanza as impassioned as "Wild nights! Wild nights!/Were I with thee,/Wild nights should be/Our luxury!" For some of the poets represented here, their love poems are among their greatest works—for instance, William Shakespeare's "Sonnet XVIII," which begins "Shall I compare thee to a summer's day," and the forty-third of Elizabeth Barrett Browning's *Sonnets from the Portuguese,* which opens with the well-known line "How do I love thee? Let me count the ways." Many of the poems collected here are among the greatest works of poetry in the English language, and they are a testament not only to romantic love but to its power to inspire our best poets to strive for the greatest heights of poetic expression.

❖

DANTE ALIGHIERI

(TRANSLATED BY DANTE GABRIEL ROSSETTI)

"My lady carries love within her eyes;"

My lady carries love within her eyes;
 All that she looks on is made pleasanter;
 Upon her path men turn to gaze at her;
He whom she greeteth feels his heart to rise,
And droops his troubled visage, full of sighs,
 And of his evil heart is then aware:
 Hate loves, and pride becomes a worshiper.
O women, help to praise her in somewise.
Humbleness, and the hope that hopeth well,
 By speech of hers into the mind are brought,
  And who beholds is blessed oftenwhiles.
  The look she hath when she a little smiles
 Cannot be said, nor holden in the thought;
'Tis such a new and gracious miracle.

"Because mine eyes can never have their fill"

Because mine eyes can never have their fill
Of looking at my lady's lovely face,
    I will so fix my gaze
That I may become blessed, beholding her
Even as an angel, up at his great height
Standing amid the light,
    Becometh blessed by only seeing God:—
So, though I be a simple earthly wight,
Yet none the less I might,
    Beholding her who is my heart's dear load,
    Be blessed, and in the spirit soar abroad.
Such power abideth in that gracious one;
Albeit felt of none
    Save of him who, desiring, honours her.

❖

SIR THOMAS WYATT

The Faithful Lover

GIVETH TO HIS MISTRESS HIS HEART
AS HIS BEST FRIEND AND ONLY TREASURE

To seek each where where man doth live,
The sea, the land, the rock, the clive,
France, Spain, and Inde, and every where;
Is none a greater gift to give,
Less set by oft, and is so lief and dear,
Dare I well say, than that I give to year.

    I cannot give broaches nor rings,
These goldsmith work, and goodly things,
Pierrie, nor pearl, orient and clear;
But for all that can no man bring
Lieffer jewel unto his lady dear,
Dare I well say, than that I give to year.

    Nor I seek not to fetch it far;
Worse is it not tho' it be narr,
And as it is, it doth appear
Uncounterfeit mistrust to bar.
It is both whole, and pure, withouten peer,
Dare I will say, the gift I give to year.

To thee therefore the same retain;
The like of thee to have again
France would I give, if mine it were.
Is none alive in whom doth reign
Lesser disdain; freely therefore lo! here
Dare I well give, I say, my heart to year.

❖

EDMUND SPENSER

(FROM *AMORETTI*)

VIII

More than most fair, full of the living fire
Kindled above unto the Maker near;
No eyes but joys, in which all powers conspire
That to the world naught else be counted dear;
Through your bright beams doth not the blinded
    guest
Shoot out his darts to base affections wound;
But angels come to lead frail minds to rest
In chaste desires, on heavenly beauty bound.
You frame my thoughts, and fashion me within;
You stop my tongue, and teach my heart to speak;
You calm the storm that passion did begin,
Strong through your cause, but by your virtue weak.
    Dark is the world, where your light shinèd never;
    Well is he born that may behold you ever.

LXX

Fresh Spring, the herald of love's mighty king,
In whose coat-armor richly are displayed
All sorts of flowers the which on earth do spring

In goodly colors gloriously arrayed;
Go to my love, where she is careless laid,
Yet in her winter's bower not well awake;
Tell her the joyous time will not be stayed,
Unless she do him by the forelock take;
Bid her therefore herself soon ready make
To wait on Love amongst his lovely crew;
Where everyone that misseth then her mate
Shall be by him amerced with penance due,

>Make haste, therefore, sweet love, whilst it is
>   prime;
>For none can call again the passèd time.

LXXV

One day I wrote her name upon the strand,
But came the waves and washèd it away:
Again I wrote it with a second hand,
But came the tide and made my pains his prey.
"Vain man," said she, "that dost in vain essay
A mortal thing so to immortalize;
For I myself shall like to this decay,
And eke my name be wipèd out likewise."
"Not so," quoth I; "let baser things devise
To die in dust, but you shall live by fame;
My verse your virtues rare shall eternize,
And in the heavens write your glorious name:

>Where, whenas Death shall all the world subdue,
>Our love shall live, and later life renew."

❖

SIR PHILIP SIDNEY

(FROM *ARCADIA*)

"My true-love hath my heart, and I have his,"

My true-love hath my heart, and I have his,
    By just exchange, one for the other given:
I hold his dear, and mine he cannot miss;
    There never was a bargain better driven:
His heart in me keeps him and me in one,
    My heart in him his thoughts and senses guides:
He loves my heart, for once it was his own,
    I cherish his, because in me it bides.

His heart his wound receivèd from my sight;
    My heart was wounded with his wounded heart;
For as from me, on him his hurt did light,
    So still me thought in me his heart did smart:
Both equal hurt, in this change sought our bliss,
    My true love hath my heart, and I have his.

(FROM *ASTROPHEL AND STELLA*)

LXII

Late tired with woe, even ready for to pine
With rage of love, I called my Love unkind;
She in whose eyes love, though unfelt, doth shine,
Sweet said that I true love in her should find.
I joyed; but straight thus watered was my wine,
That love she did, but loved a love not blind;
Which would not let me, whom she loved, decline
From nobler cause, fit for my birth and mind:
And therefore, by her love's authority,
Willed me these tempests of vain love to fly,
And anchor fast myself on Virtue's shore.
Alas, if this the only metal be
Of love new-coined to help my beggary,
Dear! love me not, that ye may love me more!

CVII

Stella! since thou so right a Princess art
Of all the powers which life bestows on me,
That ere by them aught undertaken be,
They first resort unto that sovereign part;
Sweet! for a while give respite to my heart,
Which pants as though it still should leap to thee;
And on my thoughts give thy lieutenancy
To this great cause, which needs both use and art.
And as a Queen, who from her presence sends

Whom she employs, dismiss from thee my wit,
Till it have wrought what thy own will attends:
On servants' shame oft master's blame doth sit.
O, let not fools in me thy works reprove,
And scorning, say, "See what it is to love!"

SIR WALTER RALEIGH

The Silent Lover

Wrong not, sweet mistress of my heart,
    The merit of true passion,
With thinking that he feels no smart
    Who sues for no compassion.

Since if my plaints were not t' approve
    The conquest of thy beauty,
It comes not from defect of love,
    But fear t' exceed my duty.

For, knowing that I sue to serve
    A saint of such perfection
As all desire but none deserve
    A place in her affection,

I rather choose to want relief
    Than venture the revealing:—
Where glory recommends the grief,
    Despair disdains the healing.

Thus those desires that boil so high
    In any mortal lover,
When reason cannot make them die
    Discretion them must cover.

Yet when discretion doth bereave
    The plaints that I should utter,
Then your discretion may perceive
    That silence is a suitor.

Silence in love bewrays more woe
    Than words, though ne'er so witty:
A beggar that is dumb, you know,
    May challenge double pity.

Then wrong not, dearest to my heart,
    My love, for secret passion:
He smarteth most that hides his smart,
    And sues for no compassion.

❖

WILLIAM SHAKESPEARE

Sonnet XVIII

Shall I compare thee to a summer's day?
Thou art more lovely and more temperate:
Rough winds do shake the darling buds of May,
And summer's lease hath all too short a date:
Sometime too hot the eye of heaven shines,
And often is his gold complexion dimm'd;
And every fair from fair sometime declines,
By chance or nature's changing course untrimm'd;
But thy eternal summer shall not fade
Nor lose possession of that fair thou ow'st;
Nor shall death brag thou wander'st in his shade,
When in eternal lines to time thou grow'st;
    So long as men can breathe or eyes can see,
    So long lives this, and this gives life to thee.

Sonnet XLVI

Mine eye and heart are at a mortal war,
How to divide the conquest of thy sight;
Mine eye my heart thy picture's sight would bar,
My heart mine eye the freedom of that right.

My heart doth plead that thou in him dost lie,—
A closet never pierc'd with crystal eyes,—
But the defendant doth that plea deny,
And says in him thy fair appearance lies.
To 'cide this title is impanelled
A quest of thoughts, all tenants to the heart,
And by their verdict is determined
The clear eye's moiety and the dear heart's part;
    As thus; mine eye's due is thy outward part,
    And my heart's right thy inward love of heart.

Sonnet LXVI

Tir'd with all these, for restful death I cry
As to behold desert a beggar born,
And needy nothing trimm'd in jollity,
And purest faith unhappily forsworn,
And gilded honour shamefully misplac'd,
And maiden virtue rudely strumpeted,
And right perfection wrongfully disgrac'd,
And strength by limping sway disabled,
And art made tongue-tied by authority,
And folly—doctor-like—controlling skill,
And simple truth miscall'd simplicity,
And captive good attending captain ill;
    Tir'd with all these, from these would I be gone,
    Save that, to die, I leave my love alone.

Sonnet LXXIII

That time of year thou mayst in me behold
When yellow leaves, or none, or few, do hang
Upon those boughs which shake against the cold,
Bare ruin'd choirs, where late the sweet birds sang.
In me thou see'st the twilight of such day
As after sunset fadeth in the west;
Which by and by black night doth take away,
Death's second self, that seals up all in rest.
In me thou see'st the glowing of such fire
That on the ashes of his youth doth lie,
As the death-bed whereon it must expire,
Consum'd with that which it was nourish'd by.
    This thou perceiv'st, which makes thy love more
        strong,
    To love that well which thou must leave ere long.

Sonnet CXVI

Let me not to the marriage of true minds
Admit impediments. Love is not love
Which alters when it alteration finds,
Or bends with the remover to remove:
O, no! it is an ever-fixed mark,
That looks on tempests and is never shaken;
It is the star to every wandering bark,
Whose worth's unknown, although his height
    be taken.

Love's not Time's fool, though rosy lips and cheeks
Within his bending sickle's compass come;
Love alters not with his brief hours and weeks,
But bears it out even to the edge of doom.
    If this be error and upon me prov'd,
    I never writ, nor no man ever lov'd.

Sonnet CXXX

My mistress' eyes are nothing like the sun;
Coral is far more red than her lips' red:
If snow be white, why then her breasts are dun;
If hairs be wires, black wires grow on her head.
I have seen roses damask'd, red and white,
But no such roses see I in her cheeks;
And in some perfumes is there more delight
Than in the breath that from my mistress reeks.
I love to hear her speak, yet well I know
That music hath a far more pleasing sound:
I grant I never saw a goddess go;
My mistress, when she walks, treads on the ground:
    And yet, by heaven, I think my love as rare
    As any she belied with false compare.

THOMAS CAMPION

"Love me or not, love her I must or die;"

Love me or not, love her I must or die;
Leave her or not, follow her needs must I.
O that her grace would my wished comforts give!
How rich in her, how happy should I live!

All my desire, all my delight should be
Her to enjoy, her to unite to me;
Envy should cease, her would I love alone:
Who loves by looks, is seldom true to one.

Could I enchant, and that it lawful were,
Her would I charm softly that none should hear;
But love enforced rarely yields firm content:
So would I love that neither should repent.

"There is none, O none but you,"

There is none, O none but you,
    That from me estrange the sight,
Whom mine eyes affect to view,
    Or chained ears hear with delight.

Other beauties others move:
    In you I all graces find;
Such is the effect of Love,
    To make them happy that are kind.

Women in frail beauty trust,
    Only seem your fair to me:
Still prove truly kind and just,
    For that may not dissembled be.

Sweet, afford me then your sight,
    That surveying all your looks,
Endless volumes I may write,
    And fill the world with envied books:

Which, when after-ages view,
    All shall wonder and despair,—
Woman, to find a man so true,
    Or man, a woman half so fair!

"There is a garden in her face,"

There is a garden in her face,
    Where roses and white lilies blow;
A heavenly paradise is that place,
    Wherein all pleasant fruits do grow:
        There cherries grow that none may buy.
        Till "Cherry-ripe" themselves do cry.

Those cherries fairly do enclose
    Of orient pearl a double row,
Which when her lovely laughter shows,
    They look like rosebuds tilled with snow;
        Yet them no peer nor prince may buy,
        Till "Cherry-ripe" themselves do cry.

Her eyes like angels watch them still;
    Her brows like bended bows do stand,
Threatening with piercing frowns to kill
    All that attempt with eye or hand
        These sacred cherries to come nigh,
        Till "Cherry-ripe" themselves do cry.

❖

THOMAS CAREW

Song

PERSUASIONS TO ENJOY

If the quick spirits in your eye
Now languish and anon must die;
If every sweet and every grace
Must fly from that forsaken face:
    Then, Celia, let us reap our joys
    Ere Time such goodly fruit destroys.

Or if that golden fleece must grow
For ever free from agèd snow;
If those bright suns must know no shade,
Nor your fresh beauties ever fade:
    Then fear not, Celia, to bestow
    What, still being gathered, still must grow.

Thus either Time his sickle brings
In vain, or else in vain his wings.

Song

MEDIOCRITY IN LOVE REJECTED

Give me more love, or more disdain:
    The torrid, or the frozen zone
Bring equal ease unto my pain;
    The temperate afford me none:
Either extreme of love or hate,
Is sweeter than a calm estate.

Give me a storm; if it be love,
    Like Danaë in that golden shower,
I swim in pleasure; if it prove
    Disdain, that torrent will devour
My vulture-hopes; and he's possessed
Of heaven, that's but from hell released.

The crown my joys, or cure my pain:
Give me more love, or more disdain.

❖

BEN JONSON

To Celia

Drink to me only with thine eyes,
 And I will pledge with mine;
Or leave a kiss but in the cup,
 And I'll not look for wine.
The thirst, that from the soul doth rise,
 Doth ask a drink divine:
But might I of Jove's nectar sup,
 I would not change for thine.

I sent thee late a rosy wreath,
 Not so much honouring thee,
As giving it a hope, that there
 It could not wither'd be.
But thou thereon didst only breathe,
 And sent'st it back to me:
Since when it grows, and smells, I swear,
 Not of itself, but thee.

"Kiss me, sweet: the wary lover"

Kiss me, sweet: the wary lover
Can your favors keep, and cover,
When the common courting jay
All your bounties will betray.
Kiss again! no creature comes;
Kiss, and score up wealthy sums
On my lips, thus hardly sundered
While you breathe. First give a hundred,
Then a thousand, then another
Hundred, then unto the other
Add a thousand and so more;
Till you equal with the store,
All the grass that Romney yields,
Or the sands in Chelsea fields,
Or the drops in silver Thames,
Or the stars that gild his streams
In the silent summer-nights,
When youths ply their stolen delights;
That the curious may not know
How to tell 'em as they flow,
And the envious, when they find
What their number is, be pined.

❖

JOHN DONNE

The Good-Morrow

I wonder, by my troth, what thou and I,
Did, till we loved? were we not weaned till then
But sucked on country pleasures childishly?
Or slumbered we in the Seven Sleepers' den?
'Twas so; but this, all pleasures fancies be:
If ever any beauty I did see,
Which I desired and got, 'twas but a dream of thee.

And now good-morrow to our waking souls,
Which watch not one another out of fear;
For love all love of other sights controls,
And makes one little room an everywhere.
Let sea-discoverers to new worlds have gone,
Let maps to other, worlds on worlds have shown,
Let us possess one world; each hath one, and is one.

My face in thine eye, thine in mine appears,
And true plain hearts do in the faces rest;
Where can we find two fitter hemispheres
Without sharp north, without declining west?
Whatever dies, was not mixed equally;
If our two loves be one, both thou and I
Love just alike in all, none of these loves can die.

Love's Growth

I scarce believe my love to be so pure
    As I had thought it was,
    Because it doth endure
Vicissitude and season, as the grass;
Methinks I lied all winter, when I swore
My love was infinite, if spring make it more.

But if this medicine Love, which cures all sorrow
With more, not only be no quintessence,
But mixt of all stuffs, vexing soul or sense,
And of the sun his active vigor borrow,
Love's not so pure an abstract, as they use
To say, which have no mistress but their muse;
But, as all else, being elemented too,
Love sometimes would contemplate, sometimes do.

And yet no greater, but more eminent
    Love by the spring is grown;
    As in the firmament
Stars by the sun are not enlarged, but shown.
Gentle love-deeds, as blossoms on a bough,
From Love's awakened root do bud out now.

If, as in water stirred, more circles be
Produced by one, Love such additions take,
Those, like so many spheres, but one heaven make,
For they are all concentric unto thee;
And though each spring do add to love new heat,
As princes do in times of action get

New taxes, and remit them not in peace,
No winter shall abate this spring's increase.

The Dream

Dear Love, for nothing less than thee
Would I have broke this happy dream;
    It was a theme
For reason, much too strong for phantasy,
Therefore thou waked'st me wisely; yet
My dream thou brok'st not, but continued'st it:
Thou art so true, that thoughts of thee suffice
To make dreams truths, and fables histories;
Enter these arms, for since thou thought'st it best
Not to dream all my dream, let's act the rest.

As lightning or a taper's light,
Thine eyes, and not thy noise waked me;
    Yet I thought thee
(For thou lov'st truth) an angel at first sight;
But when I saw thou saw'st my heart,
And knew'st my thoughts beyond an angel's art,
When thou knew'st what I dreamt, then thou knew'st
    when
Excess of joy would wake me, and cam'st then;
I must confess, it could not choose but be
Profane to think thee any thing but thee.

Coming and staying showed thee thee;
But rising makes me doubt that now
    Thou art not thou.

That Love is weak, where fear's as strong as he;
'Tis not all spirit, pure and brave,
If mixture it of fear, shame, honor, have.
Perchance as torches, which must ready be,
Men light and put out, so thou deal'st with me,
Thou cam'st to kindle, goest to come: then I
Will dream that hope again, but else would die.

❖

GEORGE WITHER

On a Stolen Kiss

Now gentle sleep hath closed up those eyes
Which, waking, kept my boldest thoughts in awe;
And free access unto that sweet lip lies,
From whence I long the rosy breath to draw.
Methinks no wrong it were if I should steal
From those two melting rubies one poor kiss:
None sees the theft that would the theft reveal,
Nor rob I her of aught what she can miss;
Nay, should I twenty kisses take away
There would be little sign I would do so.
Why then should I this robbery delay?
O, she may wake, and therewith angry grow!
Well, if she do, I'll back restore that one,
And twenty hundred thousand more for loan.

ROBERT HERRICK

To Ænone

What conscience, say, is it in thee,
    When I a heart had one,
To take away that heart from me,
    And to retain thy own?

For shame or pity now incline
    To play a loving part;
Either to send me kindly thine,
    Or give me back my heart.

Covet not both; but if thou dost
    Resolve to part with neither,
Why, yet to show that thou art just,
    Take me and mine together!

To Anthea, Who May Command Him Anything

Bid me to live, and I will live
 Thy Protestant to be;
Or bid me love, and I will give
 A loving heart to thee.

A heart as soft, a heart as kind,
 A heart as sound and free
As in the whole world thou canst find.
 That heart I'll give to thee.

Bid that heart stay, and it will stay
 To honor thy decree;
Or bid it languish quite away,
 And 't shall do so for thee.

Bid me to weep, and I will weep,
 While I have eyes to see;
And having none, yet I will keep
 A heart to weep for thee.

Bid me despair, and I'll despair,
 Under that cypress tree;
Or bid me die, and I will dare
 E'en death, to die for thee.

Thou art my life, my love, my heart,
 The very eyes of me;
And hast command of every part,
 To live and die for thee.

The Bracelet: To Julia

Why I tie about thy wrist,
Julia, this silken twist;
For what other reason is't
But to show thee how, in part,
Thou my pretty captive art?
But thy bond-slave is my heart:
'Tis but silk that bindeth thee,
Snap the thread and thou art free;
But 'tis otherwise with me:
I am bound and fast bound, so
That from thee I cannot go;
If I could, I would not so.

❖

SIR JOHN SUCKLING

"When, dearest, I but think of thee,"

When, dearest, I but think of thee,
Methinks all things that lovely be
    Are present, and my soul delighted:
For beauties that from worth arise
Are like the grace of deities,
    Still present thus, though unsighted.

Thus while I sit and sigh the day
With all his borrowed lights away,
    Till's nights black wings do overtake me,
Thinking on thee, thy beauties then,
As sudden lights do sleepy men,
    So they by their bright rays awake me.

Thus absence dies, and dying proves
No absence can subsist with loves
    That do partake of perfection:
Since in the darkest night they may
By love's quick motion find a way
    To see each other by reflection.

The waving sea can with each flood
Bathe some high promont that hath stood
    Far from the main up in the river:
O think not then but love can do
As much! For that's an ocean too,
    Which flows not every day, but ever!

❖

RICHARD CRASHAW

Love's Horoscope

Love, brave Virtue's younger brother,
Erst hath made my heart a mother,
She consults the conscious spheres,
To calculate her young son's years;
She asks if sad, or saving powers,
Gave omen to his infant hours;
She asks each star that then stood by,
If poor Love shall live or die.

Ah, my heart, is that the way?
Are these the beams that rule thy day?
Thou know'st a face in whose each look,
Beauty lays ope Love's fortune-book,
On whose fair revolutions wait
The obsequious motions of Love's fate.
Ah, my heart! her eyes and she
Have taught thee new astrology.
Howe'er Love's native hours were set,
Whatever starry synod met,
'Tis in the mercy of her eye,
If poor Love shall live or die.

If those sharp rays, putting on
Points of death, bid Love be gone;—
Though the Heavens in council sate
To crown an uncontrollèd fate;
Though their best aspects twined upon
The kindest constellation,
Cast amorous glances on his birth,
And whisper'd the confed'rate earth
To pave his paths with all the good
That warms the bed of youth and blood:—
Love has no plea against her eye;
Beauty frowns, and Love must die.

But if her milder influence move,
And gild the hopes of humble Love;—
Though heaven's inauspicious eye
Lay black on Love's nativity;
Though ev'ry diamond in Jove's crown
Fix'd his forehead to a frown;—
Her eye a strong appeal can give,
Beauty smiles, and Love shall live.

O, if Love shall live, O where,
But in her eye, or in her ear,
In her breast, or in her breath,
Shall I hide poor Love from death?
In the life aught else can give,
Love shall die, although he live.

Or, if Love shall die, O where,
But in her eye, or in her ear,
In her breath, or in her breast,
Shall I build his funeral nest?
While Love shall thus entombèd lie,
Love shall live, although he die!

❖

RICHARD LOVELACE

To Althea, from Prison

When love with unconfinèd wings
    Hovers within my gates,
And my divine Althea brings
    To whisper at the grates;
When I lie tangled in her hair
    And fettered to her eye,
The birds that wanton in the air
    Know no such liberty.

When flowing cups run swiftly round
    With no allaying Thames,
Our careless heads with roses bound,
    Our hearts with loyal flames;
When thirsty grief in wine we steep,
    When healths and draughts go free—
Fishes that tipple in the deep
    Know no such liberty.

When, like committed linnets, I
    With shriller throat shall sing
The sweetness, mercy, majesty,
    And glories of my King;
When I shall voice aloud how good
    He is, how great should be,
Enlargèd winds, that curl the flood,
    Know no such liberty.

Stone walls do not a prison make,
    Nor iron bars a cage;
Minds innocent and quiet take
    That for an hermitage;
If I have freedom in my love
    And in my soul am free,
Angels alone, that soar above,
    Enjoy such liberty.

❖

ANDREW MARVELL

The Definition of Love

I

My Love is of a birth as rare
As 'tis, for object, strange and high;
It was begotten by despair,
Upon impossibility.

II

Magnanimous despair alone
Could show me so divine a thing,
Where feeble hope could ne'er have flown,
But vainly flapped its tinsel wing.

III

And yet I quickly might arrive
Where my extended soul is fixed;
But fate does iron wedges drive,
And always crowds itself betwixt.

IV

For fate with jealous eye does see
Two perfect loves, nor lets them close;
Their union would her ruin be,
And her tyrannic power depose.

V

And therefore her decrees of steel
Us as the distant poles have placed,
(Though Love's whole world on us doth
    wheel)
Not by themselves to be embraced,

VI

Unless the giddy heaven fall,
And earth some new convulsion tear,
And, us to join, the world should all
Be cramped into a planisphere.

VII

As lines, so loves oblique may well
Themselves in every angle greet:
But ours, so truly parallel,
Though infinite, can never meet.

VIII

Therefore the love which us doth bind,
But fate so enviously debars,
Is the conjunction of the mind,
And opposition of the stars.

To His Coy Mistress

Had we but world enough and time,
This coyness, lady, were no crime.
We would sit down and think which way
To walk, and pass our long love's day.
Thou by the Indian Ganges' side
Shouldst rubies find: I by the tide
Of Humber would complain. I would
Love you ten years before the flood,
And you should, if you please, refuse
Till the conversion of the Jews;
My vegetable love should grow
Vaster than empires and more slow;
An hundred years should go to praise
Thine eyes, and on thy forehead gaze;
Two hundred to adore each breast,
But thirty thousand to the rest;
An age at least to every part,
And the last age should show your heart.
For, lady, you deserve this state,
Nor would I love at lower rate.

But at my back I always hear
Time's wingèd chariot hurrying near,
And yonder all before us lie
Deserts of vast eternity.
Thy beauty shall no more be found,
Nor in thy marble vault shall sound
My echoing song: then worms shall try

That long-preserved virginity,
And your quaint honour turn to dust,
And into ashes all my lust:
The grave's a fine and private place,
But none, I think, do there embrace.

Now, therefore, while the youthful hue
Sits on thy skin like morning dew,
And while thy willing soul transpires
At every pore with instant fires,
Now, let us sport us while we may,
And now, like amorous birds of prey
Rather at once our time devour,
Than languish in his slow-chaped power.
Let us roll all our strength and all
Our sweetness up into one ball,
And tear our pleasures with rough strife,
Thorough the iron gates of life;
Thus, though we cannot make our sun
Stand still, yet we will make him run.

❖

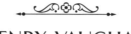

HENRY VAUGHAN

A Song to Amoret

If I were dead, and, in my place,
 Some fresher youth designed
To warm thee, with new fires; and grace
 Those arms I left behind:

Were he as faithful as the Sun,
 That's wedded to the Sphere;
His blood as chaste and temperate run,
 As April's mildest tear;

Or were he rich; and, with his heap
 And spacious share of earth,
Could make divine affection cheap,
 And court his golden birth;

For all these arts, I'd not believe
 (No! though he should be thine!),
The mighty Amorist could give
 So rich a heart as mine!

Fortune and beauty thou might'st find,
    And greater men than I;
But my true resolvèd mind
    They never shall come nigh.

For I not for an hour did love,
    Or for a day desire,
But with my soul had from above
    This endless holy fire.

❖

RICHARD BRINSLEY SHERIDAN

Love for Love

I ne'er could any lustre see
In eyes that would not look on me;
I ne'er saw nectar on a lip
But where mine own did hope to sip.
Has the maid who seeks my heart
Cheeks of rose, untouched by art?
I will own the color true
When yielding blushes aid their hue.

Is her hand so soft and pure?
I must press it to be sure;
Nor can I be certain then,
Till it, grateful, press again.
Must I, with attentive eye,
Watch her heaving bosom sigh?
I will do so when I see
That heaving bosom sigh for me.

ROBERT BURNS

Peggy's Charms

My Peggy's face, my Peggy's form,
The frost of hermit age might warm;
My Peggy's worth, my Peggy's mind,
Might charm the first of human kind.
I love my Peggy's angel air,
Her face so truly heavenly fair,
Her native grace so void of art,
But I adore my Peggy's heart.

The lily's hue, the rose's dye,
The kindling lustre of an eye;
Who but owns their magic sway?
Who but knows they all decay?
The tender thrill, the pitying tear,
The generous purpose, nobly dear,
The gentle look, that rage disarms—
These are all immortal charms.

"Come, let me take thee to my breast,"

Come, let me take thee to my breast,
　　And pledge we ne'er shall sunder;
And I shall spurn, as vilest dust,
　　The warld's wealth and grandeur:

And do I hear my Jeanie own
　　That equal transports move her?
I ask for dearest life alone,
　　That I may live to love her.

Thus in my arms, wi' a' thy charms,
　　I clasp my countless treasure;
I'll seek nae mair o' heaven to share,
　　Than sic a moment's pleasure:

And by thy een, sae bonnie blue,
　　I swear I'm thine for ever!
And on thy lips I seal my vow,
　　And break it shall I never!

Bonnie Bell

The smiling Spring comes in rejoicing,
　　And surly Winter grimly flies:
Now crystal clear are the falling waters,
　　And bonnie blue are the sunny skies;
Fresh o'er the mountains breaks forth the
　　morning,
　　The ev'ning gilds the ocean's swell,
All creatures joy in the sun's returning,

And I rejoice in my bonnie Bell.

The flowery Spring leads sunny Summer,
    And yellow Autumn presses near,
Then in his turn comes gloomy Winter,
    Till smiling Spring again appear.
Thus seasons dancing, life advancing,
    Old Time and Nature their changes tell,
But never ranging, still unchanging,
    I adore my bonnie Bell.

A Red, Red Rose

O, my luve's like a red, red rose,
    That's newly sprung in June:
O, my luve's like the melodie
    That's sweetly play'd in tune.

As fair art thou, my bonnie lass,
    So deep in luve am I:
And I will luve thee still, my dear,
    Till a' the seas gang dry.

Till a' the seas gang dry, my dear,
    And the rocks melt wi' the sun:
I will luve thee still, my dear,
    While the sands of life shall run.

And fare thee weel, my only luve!
    And fare thee weel a while!
And I will come again, my luve,
    Tho' it were ten thousand mile.

WILLIAM WORDSWORTH

"She was a Phantom of delight"

She was a Phantom of delight
When first she gleamed upon my sight;
A lovely Apparition, sent
To be a moment's ornament;
Her eyes as stars of Twilight fair;
Like Twilight's, too, her dusky hair;
But all things else about her drawn
From May-time and the cheerful Dawn;
A dancing Shape, an Image gay,
To haunt, to startle, and waylay.

I saw her upon nearer view,
A Spirit, yet a Woman too!
Her household motions light and free,
And steps of virgin liberty;
A countenance in which did meet
Sweet records, promises as sweet;
A Creature, not too bright or good
For human nature's daily food;
For transient sorrows, simple wiles,
Praise, blame, love, kisses, tears, and smiles.

And now I see with eye serene
The very pulse of the machine;
A Being breathing thoughtful breath,
A Traveller between life and death;
The reason firm, the temperate will,
Endurance, foresight, strength, and skill;
A perfect Woman, nobly planned,
To warn, to comfort, and command;
And yet a Spirit still, and bright
With something of an angel light.

❖

SAMUEL TAYLOR COLERIDGE

Love

All thoughts, all passions, all delights,
Whatever stirs this mortal frame.
All are but ministers of Love,
    And feed his sacred flame.

Oft in my waking dreams do I
Live o'er again that happy hour,
When midway on the mount I lay,
    Beside the ruined tower.

The moonshine, stealing o'er the scene
Had blended with the lights of eve;
And she was there, my hope, my joy,
    My own dear Genevieve!

She leant against the armed man,
The statue of the armed knight;
She stood and listened to my lay,
    Amid the lingering light.

Few sorrows hath she of her own,
My hope! my joy! my Genevieve!
She loves me best, whene'er I sing
    The songs that make her grieve.

I played a soft and doleful air;
I sang an old and moving story—
An old rude song, that suited well
    That ruin wild and hoary.

She listened with a flitting blush,
With downcast eyes and modest grace;
For well she knew, I could not choose
    But gaze upon her face.

I told her of the knight that wore
Upon his shield a burning brand;
And that for ten long years he wooed
    The Lady of the Land.

I told her how he pined,—and ah!
The deep, the low, the pleading tone
With which I sang another's love,
    Interpreted my own.

She listened with a flitting blush,
With downcast eyes, and modest grace;
And she forgave me, that I gazed
    Too fondly on her face!

But when I told the cruel scorn
That crazed that bold and lovely knight,
And that he crossed the mountain-woods,
    Nor rested day nor night;

That sometimes from the savage den,
And sometimes from the darksome shade,
And sometimes starting up at once
    In green and sunny glade,

There came and looked him in the face,
An angel beautiful and bright;
And that he knew it was a fiend,
　　This miserable Knight!

And that, unknowing what he did,
He leaped amid a murderous band,
And saved from outrage worse than death
　　The Lady of the Land;

And how she wept, and clasped his knees;
And how she tended him in vain,
And ever strove to expiate
　　The scorn that crazed his brain;

And that she nursed him in a cave;
And how his madness went away,
When on the yellow forest-leaves
　　A dying man he lay.

His dying words—but when I reached
That tenderest strain of all the ditty,
My faltering voice and pausing harp
　　Disturbed her soul with pity!

All impulses of soul and sense
Had thrilled my guileless Genevieve:
The music and the doleful tale,
　　The rich and balmy eve;

And hopes, and fears that kindle hope,
An undistinguishable throng,
And gentle wishes long subdued,
    Subdued and cherished long!

She wept with pity and delight,
She blushed with love, and virgin shame;
And like the murmur of a dream,
    I heard her breathe my name.

Her bosom heaved; she stepped aside,
As conscious of my look she stept;
Then suddenly, with timorous eye,
    She fled to me and wept.

She half enclosed me with her arms;
She pressed me with a meek embrace;
And bending back her head, looked up,
    And gazed upon my face.

'Twas partly love, and partly fear,
And partly 'twas a bashful art,
That I might rather feel, than see
    The swelling of her heart.

I calmed her fears, and she was calm,
And told her love with virgin pride:
And so I won my Genevieve,
    My bright and beauteous bride.

The Kiss

One kiss, dear maid! I said, and sighed:
Your scorn the little boon denied.
Ah! why refuse the blameless bliss?
Can danger lurk within a kiss?

Yon viewless wanderer of the vale,
The spirit of the western gale,
At morning's break, at evening's close,
Inhales the sweetness of the rose,
And hovers o'er the uninjured bloom,
Sighing back the soft perfume;
Vigor to the zephyr's wing
Her nectar-breathing kisses fling;
And he the glitter of the dew
Scatters on the rose's hue.
Bashful, lo! she bends her head,
And darts a blush of deeper red.

Too well those lovely lips disclose
The triumphs of the opening rose:
O fair! O graceful! bid them prove
As passive to the breath of love.
In tender accents, faint and low,
Well pleased, I hear the whispered "No!"

The whispered "No!"—how little meant!
Sweet falsehood that endears consent!
For on those lovely lips the while
Dawns the soft relenting smile,
And tempts with feigned dissuasion coy
The gentle violence of joy.

❖

MATTHEW GREGORY LEWIS

I Never Could Love Till Now

When I gaze on a beautiful face
    Or a form which my fancy approved,
I was pleased with its sweetness and grace,
    And falsely believed that I loved.
But my heart, though I strove to deceive,
    The imposture it would not allow;
I could look, I could like, I could leave,
    But I could never love—till now.

Yet though I from others could rove,
    Now harbor no doubt of my truth,
Those flames were not lighted by love,
    They were kindled by folly and youth.
But no longer of reason bereft.
    On your hand, that pure altar, I vow,
Though I have looked, and I've liked, and have
    left—
    That I have never loved—till now.

❖

THOMAS MOORE

Echoes

How sweet the answer Echo makes
    To Music at night,
When, roused by lute or horn, she wakes,
And far away o'er lawns and lakes
    Goes answering light!

Yet Love hath echoes truer far,
    And far more sweet
Than e'er, beneath the moonlight's star,
Of horn, or lute, or soft guitar,
    The songs repeat.

'Tis when the sigh,—in youth sincere,
    And only then,—
The sigh that's breathed for one to hear,
Is by that one, that only dear,
    Breathed back again.

Love's Trifling

If in loving, singing, night and day,
We could trifle merrily life away,
Like atoms dancing in the beam,
Like day-flies skimming o'er the stream,
Or summer-blossoms, born to sigh
Their sweetness out, and die,—
How brilliant, thoughtless, side by side,
Thou and I could make our minutes glide!
No atoms ever glanced so bright,
No day-flies ever danced so light,
Nor summer blossoms mixed their sigh
So close as thou and I!

❖

LEIGH HUNT

A Love-Lesson

(FROM THE FRENCH OF CLÉMENT MAROT)

A sweet "No, no!"—with a sweet smile beneath,—
Becomes an honest girl; I'd have you learn it.
As for plain "Yes!" —it may be said, i' faith,
Too plainly, and too oft: pray, well discern it.

Not that I'd have my pleasure incomplete,
Or lose the kiss for which my lips beset you;
But that in suffering me to take it, sweet,
I'd have you say, "No, no! I will not let you!"

GEORGE GORDON, LORD BYRON

Stanzas for Music

There be none of Beauty's daughters
    With a magic like thee;
And like music on the waters
    Is thy sweet voice to me:
When, as if its sound were causing
The charmèd ocean's pausing,
The waves lie still and gleaming,
And the lulled winds seem dreaming.

And the midnight moon is weaving
    Her bright chain o'er the deep,
Whose breast is gently heaving,
    As an infant's asleep:
So the spirit bows before thee,
To listen and adore thee;
With a full but soft emotion,
Like the swell of Summer's ocean.

Stanzas Written on the Road
Between Florence and Pisa

Oh, talk not to me of a name great in story;
The days of our youth are the days of our glory;
And the myrtle and ivy of sweet two-and-twenty
Are worth all your laurels, though never so plenty.

What are garlands and crowns to the brow that is
     wrinkled?
'Tis but as a dead flower with May-dew besprinkled.
Then away with all such from the head that is
     hoary!—
What care I for the wreaths that can only give glory!

Oh FAME!—if I e'er took delight in thy praises,
'Twas less for the sake of thy high-sounding phrases
Than to see the bright eyes of the dear one discover
She thought that I was not unworthy to love her.

There chiefly I sought thee, *there* only I found thee;
Her glance was the best of the rays that surround
     thee:
When it sparkled o'er aught that was bright in my
     story,
I knew it was love, and I felt it was glory.

"She walks in beauty, like the night"

She walks in beauty, like the night
    Of cloudless climes and starry skies;
And all that's best of dark and bright
    Meet in her aspect and her eyes:
Thus mellow'd to that tender light
    Which heaven to gaudy day denies.

One shade the more, one ray the less,
    Had half impair'd the nameless grace
Which waves in every raven tress,
    Or softly lightens o'er her face;
Where thoughts serenely sweet express
    How pure, how dear their dwelling-place.

And on that cheek, and o'er that brow,
    So soft, so calm, yet eloquent,
The smiles that win, the tints that glow,
    But tell of days in goodness spent,
A mind at peace with all below,
    A heart whose love is innocent!

❖

PERCY BYSSHE SHELLEY

To —

I

One word is too often profaned
    For me to profane it,
One feeling too falsely disdained
    For thee to disdain it;
One hope is too like despair
    For prudence to smother,
And pity from thee more dear
    Than that from another.

II

I can give not what men call love,
    But wilt thou accept not
The worship the heart lifts above
    And the Heavens reject not,—
The desire of the moth for the star,
    Of the night for the morrow,
The devotion to something afar
    From the sphere of our sorrow?

From the Arabic: An Imitation

I

My faint spirit was sitting in the light
    Of thy looks, my love;
It panted for thee like the hind at noon
    For the brooks, my love.
Thy barb whose hoofs outspeed the tempest's flight
    Bore thee far from me;
My heart, for my weak feet were weary soon,
Did companion thee.

II

Ah! fleeter than the fleetest storm or steed
    Or the death they bear,
The heart which tender thought clothes like a dove
    With the wings of care;
In the battle, in the darkness, in the need,
    Shall mine cling to thee,
Nor claim one smile for all the comfort, love,
    It may bring to thee.

Good-Night

Good-night? ah! no; the hour is ill
    Which severs those it should unite;
Let us remain together still,
    Then it will be *good* night.

How can I call the lone night good,
    Though thy sweet wishes wing its flight?

Be it not said, thought, understood,
    Then it will be *good* night.

 To hearts which near each other move
    From evening close to morning light,
The night is good; because, my love,
    They never *say* good-night.

Love's Philosophy

I

The fountains mingle with the river
    And the rivers with the Ocean,
The winds of Heaven mix for ever
    With a sweet emotion;
Nothing in the world is single;
    All things by a law divine
In one spirit meet and mingle.
    Why not I with thine?—

II

See the mountains kiss high Heaven
    And the waves clasp one another;
No sister-flower would be forgiven
    If it disdained its brother;
And the sunlight clasps the earth
    And the moonbeams kiss the sea:
What is all this sweet work worth
    If thou kiss not me?

I Arise from Dreams of Thee

I arise from dreams of thee
In the first sweet sleep of night,
When the winds are breathing low,
And the stars are shining bright.
I arise from dreams of thee;
And a spirit in my feet
Has led me—who knows how?
To thy chamber window, sweet!

The wandering airs, they faint
On the dark and silent stream;
The champak odors fail
Like sweet thoughts in a dream;
The nightingale's complaint,
It dies upon her heart—
As I must die on thine,
Belovéd as thou art!

O, lift me from the grass!
I die, I faint, I fail!
Let thy love in kisses rain
On my lips and eyelids pale.
My cheek is cold and white, alas!
My heart beats loud and fast:
O, press it close to thine again,
Where it will break at last!

❖

JOHN KEATS

Sonnet

I cry your mercy—pity—love!—aye, love!
    Merciful love that tantalizes not,
One-thoughted, never-wandering, guileless love,
    Unmask'd, and being seen—without a blot!
O! let me have thee whole,—all—all—be mine!
    That shape, that fairness, that sweet minor zest
Of love, your kiss,—those hands, those eyes divine,
    That warm, white, lucent, million-pleasured
        breast,—
Yourself—your soul—in pity give me all,
Withhold no atom's atom or I die,
Or living on perhaps, your wretched thrall,
    Forget, in the mist of idle misery,
Life's purposes,—the palate of my mind
Losing its gust, and my ambition blind!

Sonnet

*(Written on a Blank Page in Shakespeare's Poems,
facing "A Lover's Complaint")*

Bright star, would I were stedfast as thou art—
    Not in lone splendour hung aloft the night
And watching, with eternal lids apart,
    Like nature's patient, sleepless Eremite,
The moving waters at their priestlike task
    Of pure ablution round earth's human shores,
Or gazing on the new soft-fallen mask
    Of snow upon the mountains and the moors—
No—yet still stedfast, still unchangeable,
    Pillow'd upon my fair love's ripening breast,
To feel for ever its soft fall and swell,
    Awake for ever in a sweet unrest,
Still, still to hear her tender-taken breath,
And so live ever—or else swoon to death.

❖

THOMAS HOOD

The Tide of Love

Still glides the gentle streamlet on,
With shifting current new and strange;
The water that is here is gone,—
But those green shadows never change.

Serene, or ruffled by the storm,
On present waves as on the past,
The mirrored grove retains its form,
The selfsame trees their semblance cast.

The hue each fleeting globule wears,
That drop bequeaths it to the next:
One picture still the surface bears,
To illustrate the murmured text.

So, love, however time may flow,
Fresh hours pursuing those that flee,
One constant image still shall show
My tide of life is true to thee.

❖

THOMAS LOVELL BEDDOES

How Many Times

How many times do I love thee, dear?
   Tell me how many thoughts there be
      In the atmosphere
      Of a new-fall'n year,
Whose white and sable hours appear
   The latest flake of Eternity:
So many times do I love thee, dear.

How many times do I love, again?
   Tell me how many beads there are
      In a silver chain
      Of the evening rain,
Unravelled from the tumbling main,
   And threading the eye of a yellow star:
So many times do I love, again.

❖

EDWARD BULWER LYTTON

When Stars Are in the Quiet Skies

When stars are in the quiet skies,
　　Then most I pine for thee;
Bend on me then thy tender eyes,
　　As stars look on the sea!
For thoughts, like waves that glide by night,
　　Are stillest when they shine;
Mine earthly love lies hushed in light
　　Beneath the heaven of thine.

There is an hour when angels keep
　　Familiar watch o'er men,
When coarser souls are wrapped in sleep —
　　Sweet spirit, meet me then!
There is an hour when holy dreams
　　Through slumber fairest glide,
And in that mystic hour it seems
　　Thou shouldst be by my side.

My thoughts of thee too sacred are
　　For daylight's common beam:
I can but know thee as my star,
　　My angel, and my dream!

When stars are in the quiet skies,
    Then most I pine for thee;
Bend on me then thy tender eyes,
    As stars look on the sea!

Root and Leaf

The love that deep within me lies,
    Unmoved abides in conscious power;
Yet in the heaven of thy sweet eyes
    It varies every hour.

A look from thee will flush the cheek,
    A word of thine awaken tears;
And ah! in all I do and speak
    How frail my love appears!

In yonder tree, beloved, whose boughs
    Are household both to earth and heaven,
Whose leaves have murmured of our vows
    To many a balmly even,

The branch that wears the liveliest green
    Is shaken by the restless bird;
The leaves that nighest heaven are seen
    By every breeze are stirred.

But storms may rise, and thunders roll,
    Nor move the giant roots below;
So, from the bases of the soul,
    My love for thee doth grow.

It seeks the heaven, and trembles there
    To every light and passing breath;
But from the heart no storm can tear
    Its rooted growth beneath.

ELIZABETH BARRETT BROWNING

(from *Sonnets from the Portuguese*)

VII

The face of all the world is changed, I think,
Since first I heard the footsteps of thy soul
Move still, oh, still, beside me, as they stole
Betwixt me and the dreadful outer brink
Of obvious death, where I, who thought to sink,
Was caught up into love, and taught the whole
Of life in a new rhythm. The cup of dole
God gave for baptism, I am fain to drink,
And praise its sweetness, Sweet, with thee anear.
The names of country, heaven, are changed away
For where thou art or shalt be, there or here;
And this . . . this lute and song . . . loved yesterday,
(The singing angels know) are only dear
Because thy name moves right in what they say.

XIV

If thou must love me, let it be for nought
Except for love's sake only. Do not say

"I love her for her smile—her look—her way
Of speaking gently,—for a trick of thought
That falls in well with mine, and certes brought
A sense of pleasant ease on such a day"—
For these things in themselves, Belovèd, may
Be changed, or change for thee,—and love, so
    wrought,
May be unwrought so. Neither love me for
Thine own dear pity's wiping my cheeks dry,—
A creature might forget to weep, who bore
Thy comfort long, and lose thy love thereby!
But love me for love's sake, that evermore
Thou mayst love on, through love's eternity.

XXVII

My own Belovèd, who hast lifted me
From this drear flat of earth where I was thrown,
And, in betwixt the languid ringlets, blown
A life-breath, till the forehead hopefully
Shines out again, as all the angels see,
Before thy saving kiss! My own, my own,
Who camest to me when the world was gone,
And I who looked for only God, found thee!
I find thee; I am safe, and strong, and glad.
As one who stands in dewless asphodel
Looks backward on the tedious time he had
In the upper life,—so I, with bosom-swell,
Make witness, here, between the good and bad,
That Love, as strong as Death, retrieves as well.

XLIII

How do I love thee? Let me count the ways.
I love thee to the depth and breadth and height
My soul can reach, when feeling out of sight
For the ends of Being and ideal Grace.
I love thee to the level of everyday's
Most quiet need, by sun and candle-light.
I love thee freely, as men strive for Right;
I love thee purely, as they turn from Praise.
I love thee with the passion put to use
In my old griefs, and with my childhood's faith.
I love thee with a love I seemed to lose
With my lost saints,—I love thee with the breath,
Smiles, tears, of all my life!—and, if God choose,
I shall but love thee better after death.

❖

EDGAR ALLAN POE

To Helen

Helen, thy beauty is to me
    Like those Nicéan barks of yore,
That gently, o'er a perfumed sea,
    The weary way-worn wanderer bore
    To his own native shore.

On desperate seas long wont to roam,
    Thy hyacinth hair, thy classic face,
Thy Naiad airs have brought me home
    To the glory that was Greece,
    And the grandeur that was Rome.

Lo! in yon brilliant window-niche
    How statue-like I see thee stand,
The agate lamp within thy hand!
    Ah, Psyche, from the regions which
    Are Holy-land!

Annabel Lee

It was many and many a year ago,
    In a kingdom by the sea,
That a maiden there lived whom you may know
    By the name of Annabel Lee;—
And this maiden she lived with no other thought
    Than to love and be loved by me.

I was a child and she was a child,
    In this kingdom by the sea;
But we loved with a love that was more than love—
    I and my Annabel Lee—
With a love that the wingéd seraphs in Heaven
    Coveted her and me.

And this was the reason that, long ago,
    In this kingdom by the sea,
A wind blew out of a cloud, chilling
    My beautiful Annabel Lee;
So that her high-born kinsmen came
    And bore her away from me,
To shut her up in a sepulchre,
    In this kingdom by the sea.

The angels, not half so happy in Heaven,
    Went envying her and me—
Yes!—that was the reason (as all men know,
    In this kingdom by the sea)
That the wind came out of the cloud by night,
    Chilling and killing my Annabel Lee.

But our love it was stronger by far than the love
    Of those who were older than we—
    Of many far wiser than we—
And neither the angels in Heaven above,
    Nor the demons down under the sea,
Can ever dissever my soul from the soul
    Of the beautiful Annabel Lee:—

For the moon never beams, without bringing me
    dreams
    Of the beautiful Annabel Lee;
And the stars never rise, but I feel the bright eyes
    Of the beautiful Annabel Lee:—
And so, all the night-tide, I lie down by the side
Of my darling—my darling—my life and my bride,
    In her sepulchre there by the sea—
    In her tomb by the sounding sea.

❖

ALFRED, LORD TENNYSON

Vivien's Song

In Love, if Love be Love, if Love be ours,
Faith and unfaith can ne'er be equal powers;
Unfaith in aught is want of faith in all.

It is the little rift within the lute
That, by and by, will make the music mute,
And, ever widening, slowly silence all:

The little rift within the lover's lute,
Or little pitted speck in garnered fruit,
That, rotting inward, slowly moulders all.

It is not worth the keeping: let it go!
But shall it? answer, darling, answer No!
And trust me not at all, or all in all.

❖

OLIVER WENDELL HOLMES

To a Lady

Strange! that one lightly whispered tone
    Is far, far sweeter unto me
Than all the sounds that kiss the earth,
    Or breathe along the sea;
But, lady, when thy voice I greet,
Not heavenly music seems so sweet.

I look upon the fair, blue skies,
    And naught but empty air I see;
But when I turn me to thine eyes,
    It seemeth unto me
Ten thousand angels spread their wings
Within those little azure rings.

The lily hath the softest leaf
    That ever western breeze hath fanned;
But thou shalt have the tender flower,
    So I may take thy hand:
That little hand to me doth yield
More joy than all the broidered field.

O lady! there be many things
    That seem right fair, below, above;
But sure not one among them all
    Is half so sweet as love.
Let us not pay our vows alone,
But join two altars both in one.

❖

ROBERT BROWNING

Love in a Life

Room after room,
I hunt the house through
We inhabit together.
Heart fear nothing, for, heart, thou shalt find her—
Let in the curtain, the couch's perfume!
As she brushed it, the cornice-wreath blossomed
    anew:
Yon looking-glass gleamed at the wave of her feather.

Yet the day wears,
And door succeeds door;
I'll try the fresh fortune—
Range the the wide house from the wing to the
    center.
Still the same chance! She goes out as I enter.
Spend my whole day in the quest,—who cares?
But 'tis twilight, you see,—with such suites to
    explore,
Such closets to search, such alcoves to importune!

Life in a Love

Escape me?
Never—
Beloved!
While I am I, and you are you,
    So long as the world contains us both,
    Me the loving and you the loth,
While the one eludes, must the other pursue.
My life is a fault at last, I fear:
    It seems too much like a fate, indeed!
    Though I do my best I shall scarce succeed.
But what if I fail of my purpose here?
It is but to keep the nerves at strain,
    To dry one's eyes and laugh at a fall,
And, baffled, get up and begin again,—
    So the chase takes up one's life, that's all.
While, look but once from your farthest bound
    At me so deep in the dust and dark,
No sooner the old hope drops to ground
    Than a new one, straight to the self-same mark,
        I shape me—
        Ever
        Removed!

Song

Nay but you, who do not love her,
    Is she not pure gold, my mistress?
Holds earth aught—speak truth—above her?
    Aught like this tress, see, and this tress,
And this last fairest tress of all,
So fair, see, ere I let it fall?

Because you spend your lives in praising;
    To praise, you search the wide world over:
Then why not witness, calmly gazing,
    If earth holds aught—speak truth—above her?
Above this tress, and this, I touch
But cannot praise, I love so much!

❖

CHARLOTTE BRONTË

Regret

Long ago I wished to leave
    "The house where I was born";
Long ago I used to grieve,
    My home seemed so forlorn.
In other years, its silent rooms
    Were filled with haunting fears;
Now their very memory comes
    O'ercharged with tender tears.

Life and marriage I have known,
    Things once deemed so bright;
Now how utterly is flown
    Every ray of light!
Mid the unknown sea of life
    I no blest isle have found;
At last, through all its wild waves strife,
    My bark is homeward bound.

Farewell, dark and rolling deep!
    Farewell, foreign shore!
Open, in unclouded sweep,
    Thou glorious realm before!
Yet, though I had safely pass'd
    That weary, vexed main,
One loved voice, through surge and blast,
    Could call me back again.

Though the soul's bright morning rose
    O'er Paradise for me,
William! even from Heaven's repose
    I'd turn, invoked by thee!
Storm nor surge should e'er arrest
    My soul, exulting then:
All my heaven was once thy breast,
    Would it were mine again!

❖

EMILY BRONTË

Remembrance

Cold in the earth—and the deep snow piled above
    thee,
Far, far, removed, cold in the dreary grave!
Have I forgot, my only Love, to love thee,
Severed at last by Time's all-severing wave?

Now, when alone, do my thoughts no longer hover
Over the mountains, on that northern shore,
Resting their wings where heath and fern-leaves
    cover
Thy noble heart for ever, ever more?

Cold in the earth—and fifteen wild Decembers,
From those brown hills, have melted into spring:
Faithful, indeed, is the spirit that remembers
After such years of change and suffering!

Sweet Love of youth, forgive, if I forget thee,
While the world's tide is bearing me along;
Other desires and other hopes beset me,
Hopes which obscure, but cannot do thee wrong!

No later light has lightened up my heaven,
No second morn has ever shone for me;
All my life's bliss from thy dear life was given,
All my life's bliss is in the grave with thee.

But, when the days of golden dreams had perished,
And even Despair was powerless to destroy;
Then did I learn how existence could be cherished,
Strengthened, and fed without the aid of joy.

Then did I check the tears of useless passion—
Weaned my young soul from yearning after thine;
Sternly denied its burning wish to hasten
Down to that tomb already more than mine.

And, even yet, I dare not let it languish,
Dare not indulge in memory's rapturous pain;
Once drinking deep of that divinest anguish,
How could I seek the empty world again?

❖

DANTE GABRIEL ROSSETTI

Love's Testament

O thou who at Love's hour ecstatically
    Unto my heart dost ever more present,
    Clothed with his fire, thy heart his testament;
Whom I have neared and felt thy breath to be
The inmost incense of his sanctuary;
    Who without speech hast owned him, and, intent
    Upon his will, thy life with mine hast blent,
And murmured, "I am thine, thou'rt one with me!"

O what from thee the grace, to me the prize,
    And what to Love the glory,—when the whole
    Of the deep stair thou tread'st to the dim shoal
And weary water of the place of sighs,
And there dost work deliverance, as thine eyes
    Draw up my prisoned spirit to thy soul!

Lovesight

When do I see thee most, beloved one?
    When in the light the spirits of mine eyes
    Before thy face, their altar, solemnize
The worship of that Love through thee made known?

Or when in the dusk hours, (we two alone,)
    Close-kissed and eloquent of still replies
    Thy twilight-hidden glimmering visage lies,
And my soul only sees thy soul its own?

O love, my love! if I no more should see
Thyself, nor on the earth the shadow of thee,
    Nor image of thine eyes in any spring,—
How then should sound upon Life's darkening slope
The ground-whirl of the perished leaves of Hope,
    The wind of Death's imperishable wing?

Mid-Rapture

Thou lovely and beloved, thou my love;
    Whose kiss seems still the first; whose summoning
        eyes,
    Even now, as for our love-world's new sunrise,
Shed very dawn; whose voice, attuned above
All modulation of the deep-bowered dove,
    Is like a hand laid softly on the soul;
    Whose hand is like a sweet voice to control
Those worn tired brows it hath the keeping of:—

What word can answer to thy word,—what gaze
    To thine, which now absorbs within its sphere
    My worshipping face, till I am mirrored there
Light-circled in a heaven of deep-drawn rays?
    What clasp, what kiss mine inmost heart can
        prove,
    O lovely and beloved, O my love?

CHRISTINA ROSSETTI

I Loved You First

I loved you first: but afterwards your love,
     Outsoaring mine, sang such a loftier song
As drowned the friendly cooings of my dove.
     Which owes the other most? My love was long,
     And yours one moment seemed to wax more
          strong;
I loved and guessed at you, you construed me
And loved me for what might or might not be—
     Nay, weights and measures do us both a wrong.
For verily love knows not "mine" or "thine";
     With separate "I" and "thou" free love has done,
          For one is both and both are one in love:
Rich love knows nought of "thine that is not mine";
          Both have the strength and both the length
               thereof,
     Both of us, of the love which makes us one.

In the Lane

When my love came home to me,
    Pleasant summer bringing.
Every tree was out in leaf,
    Every bird was singing.

There I met her in the lane
    By those waters gleamy,
Met her toward the fall of day,
    Warm and dear and dreamy.
Did I loiter in the lane?
    None was there to see me.

Only roses in the hedge,
    Lilies on the river,
Saw our greeting fast and fond,
    Counted gift and giver,
Saw me take her to my home,
    Take her home for ever.

Love from the North

I had a love in soft south land,
    Beloved through April far in May;
He waited on my lightest breath,
    And never dared to say me nay.

He saddened if my cheer were sad,
    But gay he grew if I were gay;
We never differed on a hair,
    My yes his yes, my nay his nay.

The wedding hour was come, the aisles
    We flushed with sun and flowers that day;
I pacing balanced in my thoughts:
    "It's quite too late to think of nay."—

My bridegroom answered in his turn,
    Myself had almost answered "yea":
When through the flashing nave I heard
    A struggle and resounding "nay."

Bridesmaids and bridegroom shrank in fear,
    But I stood high who stood at bay:
"And if I answer yea, fair Sir,
    What man art thou to bar with nay?"

He was a strong man from the north,
    Light-locked, with eyes of dangerous grey:
"Put yea by for another time
    In which I will not say thee nay."

He took me in his strong white arms,
    He bore me on his horse away
O'er crag, morass, and hairbreadth pass,
    But never asked me yea or nay.

He made me fast with book and bell,
    With links of love he make me stay;
Till now I've neither heart nor power
    Nor will nor wish to say him nay.

A Bride Song

Through the vales to my love!
To the happy small nest of home
Green from basement to roof;
Where the honey-bees come
To the window-sill flowers,
    And dive from above,
Safe from the spider that weaves
    Her warp and her woof
    In some outermost leaves.

Through the vales to my love!
    In sweet April hours
    All rainbows and showers,
    While dove answers dove,—
    In beautiful May,
    When the orchards are tender
    And frothing with flowers,—
    In opulent June
    When the wheat stands up slender
    By sweet-smelling hay,
    And half the sun's splendour
    Descends to the moon.

Through the vales to my love!
Where the turf is so soft to the feet
    And the thyme makes it sweet,
    And the stately foxglove
Hangs silent its exquisite bells;
    And where water wells

The greenness grows greener,
And bulrushes stand
Round a lily to screen her.

Nevertheless, if this land,
Like a garden to smell and to sight,
Were turned to a desert of sand;
    Stripped bare of delight,
    All its best gone to worst,
    For my feet no repose,
No water to comfort my thirst,
And heaven like a furnace above,—
    The desert would be
As gushing of waters to me,
The wilderness be as a rose,
    If it led me to thee,
        O my love.

At Last

Many have sung of love a root of bane:
　　While to my mind a root of balm it is,
　　For love at length breeds love; sufficient bliss
For life and death and rising up again.
Surely when light of Heaven makes all things plain,
　　Love will grow plain with all its mysteries;
　　Nor shall we need to fetch from over seas
Wisdom or wealth or pleasure safe from pain.
Love in our borders, love within our heart,
　　Love all in all, we then shall bide at rest,
　　Ended for ever life's unending quest,
　　Ended for ever effort, change, and fear:
Love all in all;—no more that better part
Purchased, but at the cost of all things here.

❖

EMILY DICKINSON

"Alter? When the hills do."

Alter? When the hills do.
Falter? When the sun
Question if his glory
Be the perfect one.

Surfeit? When the daffodil
Doth of the dew:
Even as herself, O friend!
I will of you!

"Doubt me, my dim companion!"

Doubt me, my dim companion!
Why, God would be content
With but a fraction of the love
Poured thee without a stint.
The whole of me, forever,
What more the woman can,—
Say quick, that I may dower thee
With last delight I own!

It cannot be my spirit,
For that was thine before;
I ceded all of dust I knew,—
What opulence the more
Had I, a humble maiden,
Whose farthest of degree
Was that she might,
Some distant heaven,
Dwell timidly with thee!

"If you were coming in the fall,"

If you were coming in the fall,
I'd brush the summer by
With half a smile and half a spurn,
As housewives do a fly.

If I could see you in a year,
I'd wind the months in balls,
And put them each in separate drawers,
Until their time befalls.

If only centuries delayed,
I'd count them on my hand,
Subtracting till my fingers dropped
Into Van Diemen's land.

If certain, when this life was out,
That yours and mine should be,
I'd toss it yonder like a rind,
And taste eternity.

But now, all ignorant of the length
Of time's uncertain wing,
It goads me, like the goblin bee,
That will not state its sting.

"I hide myself within my flower,"

I hide myself within my flower,
That wearing on your breast,
You, unsuspecting, wear me too—
And angels know the rest.

I hide myself within my flower,
That, fading from your vase,
You, unsuspecting, feel for me
Almost a loneliness.

"That I did always love,"

That I did always love,
I bring thee proof:
That till I loved
I did not love enough.

That I shall love alway,
I offer thee
That love is life,
And life hath immortality.

This, dost thou doubt, sweet?
Then have I
Nothing to show
But Calvary.

"I'm ceded, I've stopped being theirs;"

I'm ceded, I've stopped being theirs;
The name they dropped upon my face
With water, in the country church,
Is finished using now,
And they can put it with my dolls,
My childhood, and the string of spools
I've finished threading too.

Baptized before without the choice,
But this time consciously, of grace
Unto supremest name,
Called to my full, the crescent dropped,
Existence's whole arc filled up
With one small diadem.

My second rank, too small the first,
Crowned, crowing on my father's breast,
A half unconscious queen;
But this time, adequate, erect,
With will to choose or to reject,
And I choose—just a throne.

"'Twas a long parting, but the time"

'Twas a long parting, but the time
For interview had come;
Before the judgment-seat of God,
The last and second time

These fleshless lovers met,
A heaven in a gaze,
A heaven of heavens, the privilege
Of one another's eyes.

No lifetime set on them,
Apparelled as the new
Unborn, except they had beheld,
Born everlasting now.

Was bridal e'er like this?
A paradise, the host,
And cherubim and seraphim
The most familiar guest.

"Come slowly, Eden!"

Come slowly, Eden!
Lips unused to thee,
Bashful, sip thy jasmines,
As the fainting bee,

Reaching late his flower,
Round her chamber hums,
Counts his nectars—enters,
And is lost in balms!

"Wild nights! Wild nights!"

Wild nights! Wild nights!
Were I with thee,
Wild nights should be
Our luxury!

Futile the winds
To a heart in port,—
Done with the compass,
Done with the chart.

Rowing in Eden!
Ah! the sea!
Might I but moor
To-night in thee!

ALGERNON CHARLES SWINBURNE

Madonna Mia

Under green apple boughs
That never a storm will rouse,
My lady hath her house
    Between two bowers;
In either of the twain
Red roses full of rain;
She hath for bondwomen
    All kind of flowers.

She hath no handmaid fair
To draw her curled gold hair
Through rings of gold that bear
    Her whole hair's weight;
She hath no maids to stand
Gold-clothed on either hand;
In all that great green land
    None is so great.

She hath no more to wear
But one white hood of vair
Drawn over eyes and hair,
    Wrought with strange gold,

Made for some great queen's head,
Some fair great queen since dead;
And one strait gown of red
    Against the cold.

Beneath her eyelids deep
Love lying seems asleep,
Love, swift to wake, to weep,
    To laugh, to gaze;
Her breasts are like white birds,
All her gracious words
As water-grass to herds
    In the June-days.

To her all dews that fall
And rains are musical;
Her flowers are few from all,
    Her joys from these;
In the deep-feathered firs
Their gift of joy is hers,
In the least breath that sirs
    Across the trees.

She grows with greenest leaves,
Ripens with reddest sheaves,
Forgets, remember, grieves,
    And is not sad;
The quiet lands and skies
Leave light upon her eyes;
None knows her, weak or wise,
    Or tired or glad.

None knows, none understands,
What flowers are her hands;
Though you should search all lands
    Wherein time grows,
What snows are like her feet,
Though his eyes burn with heat
Though grazing on my sweet,—
    Yet no man knows.

Only this thing is said;
That white and gold and red,
God's three chief words, man's bread
    And oil and wine,
Were given her for dowers,
And kingdoms of all hours,
And grace of goodly flowers
    And various vine.

This is my lady's praise:
God after many days
Wrought in her unknown ways,
    In sunset lands;
This is my lady's birth;
God gave her right and mirth.
And laid his whole sweet earth
    Between her hands.

Under deep apple boughs
My lady hath her house;
She wears upon her brows
    The flower thereof;

All saying but what God saith
To her is as vain breath;
She is more strong than death,
     Being strong as love.

A Match

If love were what the rose is,
     And I were like the leaf,
Our lives would grow together
In sad or singing weather,
Blown fields or flowerful closes,
     Green pleasure or gray grief;
If love were what the rose is,
     And I were like the leaf.

If I were what the words arc,
     And love were like the tune,
With double sound and single
Delight our lips would mingle,
With kisses glad as birds are
     That get sweet rain at noon;
If I were what the words are,
     And love were like the tune.

If you were life, my darling,
     And I, your love, were death,
We'd shine and snow together
Ere March made sweet the weather
With daffodil and starling
     And hours of fruitful breath;

If you were life, my darling,
    And I, your love, were death.

If you were thrall to sorrow,
    And I were page to joy,
We'd play for lives and seasons,
With loving looks and treasons,
And tears of night and morrow,
    And laughs of maid and boy;
If you were thrall to sorrow,
    And I were page to joy.

If you were April's lady,
    And I were lord in May,
We'd throw with leaves for hours,
And draw for days with flowers,
Till day like night were shady
    And night were bright like day;
If you were April's lady,
    And I were lord in May.

If you were queen of pleasure,
    And I were king of pain,
We'd hunt down love together,
Pluck out his flying-feather,
And teach his feet a measure,
    And find his mouth a rein;
If you were queen of pleasure,
    And I were king of pain.

❖

WILLIAM BUTLER YEATS

The Lover Tells of the Rose
in His Heart

All things uncomely and broken, all things worn out
    and old,
The cry of a child by the roadway, the creak of a
    lumbering cart,
The heavy steps of the ploughman, splashing the
    wintry mould,
Are wronging your image that blossoms a rose in the
    deeps of my heart.

The wrong of unshapely things is a wrong too great
    to be told;
I hunger to build them anew and sit on a green
    knoll apart,
With the earth and the sky and the water, remade,
    like a casket of gold
For my dreams of your image that blossoms a rose in
    the deeps of my heart.

He Remembers Forgotten Beauty

When my arms wrap you round I press
My heart upon the loveliness
That has long faded from the world;
The jewelled crowns that kings have hurled
In shadowy pools, when armies fled;
The love-tales wrought with silken thread
By dreaming ladies upon cloth
That has made fat the murderous moth;
The roses that of old time were
Woven by ladies in their hair,
The dew-cold lilies ladies bore
Through many a sacred corridor
Where such gray clouds of incense rose
That only the gods' eyes did not close:
For that pale breast and lingering hand
Come from a more dream-heavy land,
A more dream-heavy hour than this;
And when you sigh from kiss to kiss
I hear white Beauty sighing, too,
For hours when all must fade like dew,
All but the flames, and deep on deep,
Throne over throne where in half sleep,
Their swords upon their iron knees,
Brood her high lonely mysteries.

Never Give All the Heart

Never give all the heart, for love
Will hardly seem worth thinking of
To passionate women if it seem
Certain, and they never dream
That it fades out from kiss to kiss;
For everything that's lovely is
But a brief dreamy kind delight.
O never give the heart outright,
For they, for all smooth lips can say,
Have given their hearts up to the play
And who could play it well enough
If deaf and dumb and blind with love?
He that made this knows all the cost,
For he gave all his heart and lost.

❖

INDEX OF FIRST LINES